MISSION CONTROL

THE VOYAGER SPACE PROBES

JENNIFER LOMBARDO

PowerKiDS
press

Published in 2025 by The Rosen Publishing Group, Inc.
2544 Clinton Street, Buffalo, NY 14224

Copyright © 2025 by The Rosen Publishing Group, Inc.

All rights reserved. No part of this book may be reproduced in any form without permission in writing from the publisher, except by a reviewer.

First Edition

Editor: Jennifer Lombardo
Book Design: Rachel Rising

Photo Credits: Cover JesperG/Shutterstock.com; cover, pp. 1, 3–32 KK.KICKIN/Shutterstock.com; p. 4 Claudio Caridi/Shutterstock.com; pp. 5, 14, 15, 21 NASA/JPL-Caltech; p. 6 buradaki/Shutterstock.com; p. 7 Matson Photo Service, photographer. Types and character, etc. Shepherd boy slinging, (A modern David). Between 1950 and 1977. Photograph. Retrieved from the Library of Congress,<www.loc.gov/item/2019705754/>; p. 8 Beyond Space/Shutterstock.com; p. 9 Lee Yiu Tung/Shutterstock.com; p. 10 Antrakt2/Shutterstock.com; p. 11 Anna Jurkovska/Shutterstock.com; pp. 13, 23 Schager/Shutterstock.com; pp. 16, 17 NASA/JPL; p. 19 https://commons.wikimedia.org/wiki/File:PIA22835-VoyagerProgram%26Heliosphere-Chart-20181210.png; p. 20 sripfoto/Shutterstock.com; p. 22 rafapress/Shutterstock.com; p. 24 ArtMediaWorx/Shutterstock.com; p. 25 Dimitrios Karamitros/Shutterstock.com; p. 26 Astrodefa87/Shutterstock.com; p. 27 Erkki Makkonen/Shutterstock.com; p. 28 Dotted Yeti/Shutterstock.com; p. 29 24K-Production/Shutterstock.com.

Library of Congress Cataloging-in-Publication Data

Names: Lombardo, Jennifer.
Title: The Voyager space probes / Jennifer Lombardo.
Description: Buffalo, NY : PowerKids Press, 2025. | Series: Mission control | Includes glossary and index.
Identifiers: ISBN 9781499449938 (pbk.) | ISBN 9781499449945 (library bound) | ISBN 9781499449952 (ebook)
Subjects: LCSH: Voyager Project--Juvenile literature. | Space probes--Juvenile literature. | Planets--Exploration--Juvenile literature.
Classification: LCC TL789.8.U6 L66 2025 | DDC 629.45'4--dc23

Manufactured in the United States of America

Some of the images in this book illustrate individuals who are models. The depictions do not imply actual situations or events.

CPSIA Compliance Information: Batch #CWPK25. For further information contact Rosen Publishing at 1-800-237-9932.

CONTENTS

A JOURNEY THROUGH SPACE 4

CAREFULLY PLANNED 6

PROBE PARTS 8

ONBOARD INSTRUMENTS 10

THE GOLDEN RECORD 12

OLD FINDINGS 14

NEW FINDINGS 18

BIG AND EMPTY 20

TROUBLESHOOTING 22

COMPARING THE VOYAGERS 24

POWERING DOWN 26

THE NEXT PROBE 28

GLOSSARY 30

FOR MORE INFORMATION 31

INDEX 32

A JOURNEY THROUGH SPACE

In 1977, NASA launched two probes: unmanned spacecraft loaded with instruments, or tools, to measure and record data in space. These probes, named Voyager 1 and Voyager 2, set off on a journey to help scientists learn about space up close. Their primary goal was to study Jupiter and Saturn.

The probes fulfilled this goal many years ago and went on to study Uranus and Neptune as well. In 2012, Voyager 1 made history by becoming the first man-made object to enter **interstellar** space. Voyager 2 followed in 2018. Both probes are still sending information back to Earth as of 2024 and are expected to continue working until at least 2030. The longer they stay operational in deep space, the more humans will learn.

NASA KNOWLEDGE

Voyager 2 was the first probe to be launched, leaving Earth on August 20. Voyager 1 followed it on September 5.

This picture from 1976 shows a NASA engineer working on part of one of the Voyager probes.

CAREFULLY PLANNED

The Voyager launches were timed to take advantage of the positions of Jupiter, Saturn, Uranus, and Neptune. The four planets were lined up in such a way that as the probes passed each one, the planet's gravity acted as a slingshot to help the probe speed up and change direction toward its next target. This is called a gravity assist.

Using gravity assist was a way to get the Voyager probes into interstellar space quickly and without using a lot of fuel. If they had not been able to use gravity assist, they would have slowed down over time. This means they would not have been able to travel nearly as far as they did in the time they've been in space.

GRAVITY ASSIST

When a small object approaches a large object, the large object's gravity pulls the small object toward it. In the case of Voyager 2 and Jupiter, for example, the planet pulled Voyager in as the probe passed behind it. This made the probe speed up. It ended up going so fast that it passed Jupiter's **escape velocity**. Instead of staying in orbit around the planet, the probe sped onward into space.

When someone uses a type of slingshot called a shepherd's sling, they whirl a rock in the sling over their head and then let it go so it flies fast and far in a certain direction. The planets acted like a shepherd's sling on the Voyager probes.

PROBE PARTS

The Voyagers were designed to be identical, or exactly the same. Each was built with a radio dish, 16 **thrusters**, and 10 scientific instruments, or tools. The radio dish transmits, or sends, information back to Earth. The thrusters control the speed and direction of the probe.

Five of the scientific instruments were included to observe and measure planets. These include cameras and **spectrometers**. Because the probes are now past all the planets in the solar system, these instruments have been shut off to save power. All five of Voyager 2's remaining instruments work, but Voyager 1 has a broken plasma spectrometer. This instrument is made to measure plasma, which is gas heated to such a high temperature that the atoms in it break apart.

NASA KNOWLEDGE

The probes run on two kinds of power. The thrusters use a kind of fuel called hydrazine, also known as rocket fuel. Each probe has a nuclear power generator that runs on plutonium. This generator powers the onboard instruments.

On Earth, these are called "satellite dishes" when they transmit information to satellites. However, the Voyager probes use radio waves to transmit information, so their instrument is called a radio dish.

ONBOARD INSTRUMENTS

In addition to the plasma spectrometer, the probes are still using four of their instruments. The first is a magnetometer, which measures magnetic fields. The second is an instrument that measures low-energy charged particles. In space, particles with an electric charge float around freely. This instrument measures the speed, direction, and number of particles in various places in space.

The third instrument measures cosmic rays. These are high-energy particles in plasma. The fourth measures plasma waves. The difference between a wave and a particle is that a particle is small, so it only affects a small space. A wave is larger and more spread out. Having two different instruments makes it easier to measure both types of plasma.

Plasma can be found on Earth as well. Many science museums have plasma balls similar to this one. These tools allow people to see how plasma behaves.

11

THE GOLDEN RECORD

The most **unique** object on each of the probes is the Golden Record. Like the probes, each copy is identical. The gold-plated record is made to be played on a phonograph, or record player. On its cover are instructions for how to build a phonograph to play the record, as well as how long the record should be when played at the correct speed. The record itself contains sounds and pictures that show what life is like on Earth.

The record is a message to any alien life the probes may encounter. It was purposely designed to only be playable if the aliens are intelligent and advanced enough to understand the directions on the cover and build their own phonograph.

NASA KNOWLEDGE

The record includes 115 pictures, greetings in more than 50 languages, and 90 minutes of music from all around the world. It also carries sounds from Earth, such as volcanoes, waves, laughter, animals, and tools.

This copy of the Golden Record is on display at NASA's Jet Propulsion Laboratory (JPL).

OLD FINDINGS

Since their launch in 1977, the Voyager probes have been changing our understanding of the solar system. For example, thanks to the pictures the probes took of Jupiter, scientists were able to study the wind patterns on that planet by watching how the clouds moved. They also discovered volcanic activity on Io, one of Jupiter's moons. This is the only place in the solar system we know of, aside from Earth, where we're sure there are active volcanoes.

The close-up pictures revealed things we could never have seen from Earth, such as rings around Jupiter. These rings are made of dust, so they're much harder to see than Saturn's rings. The Voyagers also revealed other objects that were impossible to see or measure from Earth, such as 10 extra moons and a magnetic field around Uranus.

SATURN'S RINGS

DIFFERENT TRAJECTORIES

The probes were launched at different times and were meant to take different trajectories. For a while, they followed a similar path, so both probes visited Jupiter and Saturn. After Saturn, Voyager 1's path took it out of the solar system. Voyager 2 was the only probe to visit Uranus and Neptune. Neither probe flew past Pluto. After it visited Neptune in 1989, Voyager 2 followed Voyager 1 into interstellar space.

This is one of Voyager 1's most famous pictures. It is known as the "Pale Blue Dot," and it shows Earth as it looks from the edge of the solar system—3.7 billion miles (5.9 billion km) from the sun.

At Neptune, Voyager 2 made more discoveries. The probe returned photos of three rings around Neptune that were not visible from Earth as well as those of six previously unknown moons orbiting the planet. Voyager also noted volcanic vents on Titan, one of Neptune's moons. However, while Io's volcanoes erupt with hot lava like Earth's volcanoes, scientists believe Titan's volcanoes spew ice.

The probes' magnetometers showed that all the planets they visited have a magnetic field. This means they can produce auroras. On Earth, the most famous aurora is known as the aurora borealis, or northern lights. These lights appear in the sky when solar particles interact with Earth's magnetic field. The same happens on other planets as well, but we can't see them from Earth.

TITAN'S CRYOVOLCANOES

Voyager 2 was the first probe to notice volcanic activity on Titan. A later mission called Cassini-Huygens collected much more information. Scientists know that Neptune's atmosphere has a lot of the gas called methane in it. They believe that the ice volcanoes, or cryovolcanoes, erupt with frozen methane from the planet's core. Some of this methane then turns to gas. Scientists say this could explain where all the methane in the atmosphere comes from.

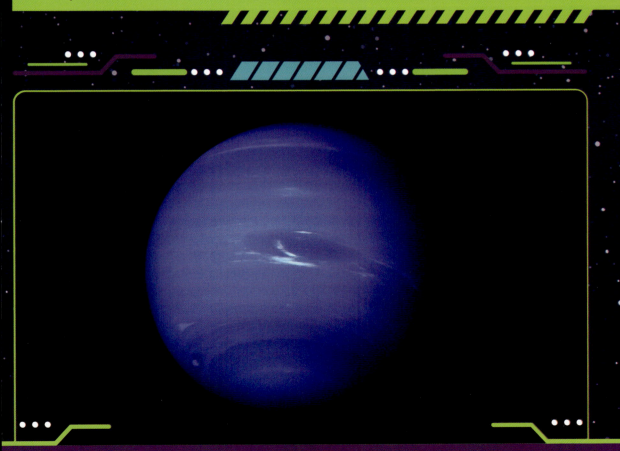

Voyager 2 took the first photos of Neptune.

NEW FINDINGS

There is much less to see in interstellar space. There are no planets or stars. However, there is activity for the probes to measure. Stars give off a stream of plasma. When it comes from our sun, this stream is called solar wind. Outside the **heliosphere**, the probes are still experiencing a little bit of solar wind. However, there is now wind from other stars affecting them as well.

Scientists are using the probes' instruments to learn more about these winds and how they interact with the interstellar **environment**. For example, Voyager 1's Plasma Wave System (PWS) has picked up bursts of activity from the sun. When there is no activity, the PWS records a very faint hum coming from the interstellar plasma.

NASA KNOWLEDGE

The hum Voyager 1 is picking up has been described by scientist James Cordes as sounding similar to a gentle rain.

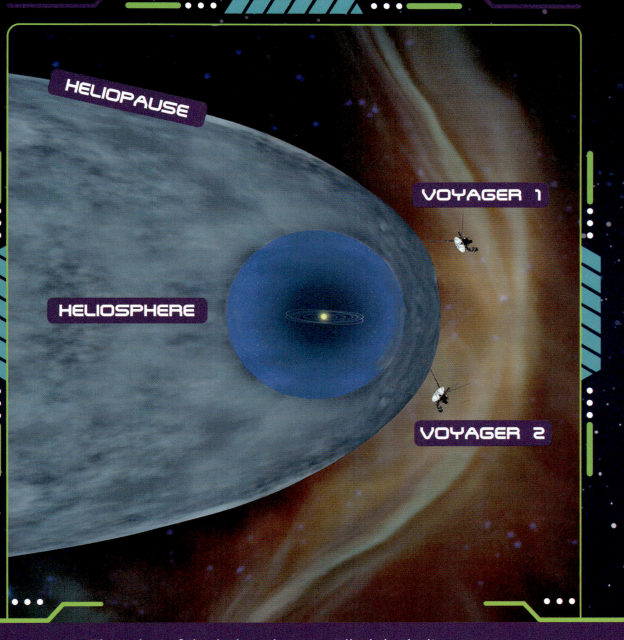

The edge of the heliosphere is called the heliopause. This picture shows how the Voyagers have crossed the heliopause into interstellar space.

BIG AND EMPTY

Studying the information Voyager 1's PWS sends back will help scientists learn more about how plasma is **distributed** across the interstellar medium. This is the first time in human history we have ever been able to study this directly.

Voyager 1 is also telling us more about how incredibly huge and empty space is. The probe travels about 900,000 miles (1.44 million km) every day. It has been in interstellar space for about 12 years, but it has not yet come anywhere close to another planet or star. In fact, NASA estimates that it will take about 40,000 years for either Voyager to get within 1.7 light-years of another star. By that time, the probes will likely no longer be working, so we may never know what they find there.

THE INTERSTELLAR MEDIUM

The interstellar medium is the name scientists have given the material that lies between stars. The Voyager probes are moving through this medium, or material. It includes clouds of gas and dust, cosmic rays, magnetic fields, and some very small solid particles. When enough of this material collects in one place, it can start to form a cloud called a nebula. Over time, if this cloud gets big and dense enough, new stars can form.

It has been many years since either Voyager probe has encountered anything to take a picture of. This picture of Ganymede, one of Jupiter's moons, was taken in 1979.

TROUBLESHOOTING

Any machine is going to have problems, and the Voyagers are no exception. In November 2023, Voyager 1 began sending **corrupted** information back to NASA. Engineers began trying to fix the probe right away, but the process took some time. Part of the reason for this is that, because of how far away the probe is now, it takes one full day to send messages to Voyager 1 and one full day to receive an answer.

By April 2024, the engineers had figured out the problem. They had Voyager 1 back up and running by June. However, Voyager 2 also had problems in 2023. NASA controls the probes with computer commands. An incorrect command sent in July made Voyager 2 point in the wrong direction, so its information was missing Earth. The problem was fixed in October.

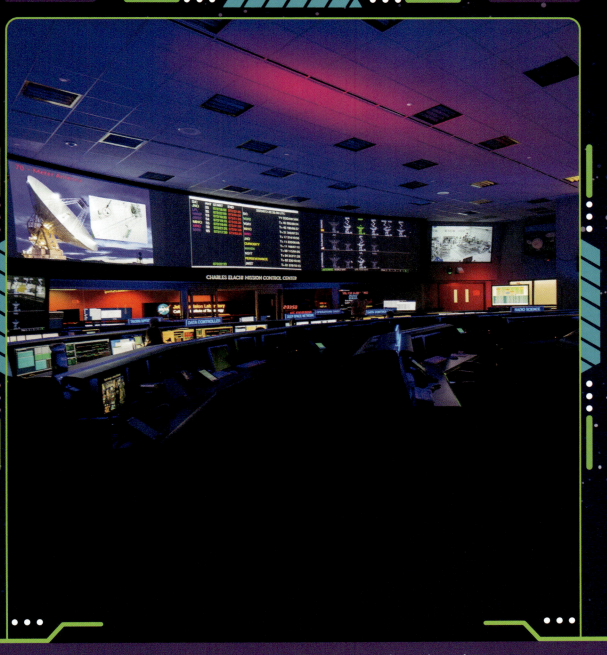

NASA controls the Voyager probes and studies their information from control rooms full of computers.

COMPARING THE VOYAGERS

Having two probes travel on similar—but not identical—trajectories has helped NASA collect even more information by comparing what each probe has encountered. Sometimes this information raises more questions than answers. For example, Voyager 1 and 2 exited the heliopause at different times and places. When Voyager 2 exited, the sun was at solar minimum. When Voyager 1 exited, it was at solar maximum.

The part that confused scientists was that both probes exited the heliopause at almost the exact same distance from the sun. They have noticed that the heliosphere gets larger at solar maximum and smaller at solar minimum.

According to what scientists thought they knew, the probes should have exited at very different distances from the sun. With this new information from the probes, they will have to reexamine how the heliosphere works.

THE SUN'S CYCLE

The sun goes through a roughly 11-year cycle of activity. Its least active time is called solar minimum. Its most active time is called solar maximum. The sun experiences explosions on its surface called solar flares. During solar maximum, these flares become larger and more frequent, reaching all the way to Earth and often causing problems with electronic and magnetic equipment.

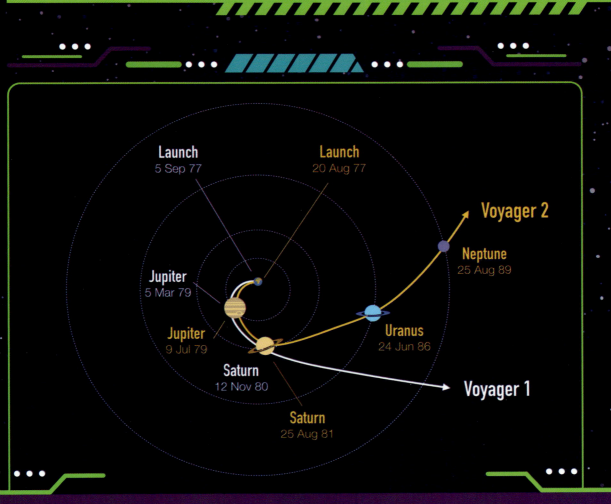

This picture shows the different trajectories of the two Voyagers.

POWERING DOWN

The Voyagers have lasted a long time, but scientists know they won't last forever. Voyager 1 is already showing signs of failing. It could use up its power supply as soon as 2025. If Voyager 2 outlasts Voyager 1, NASA plans to shut down its instruments one at a time to save power, starting in 2026. Neither probe is expected to work past 2031.

After the probes shut down, they are expected to float through space at the same rate and trajectory they are currently traveling. They will not be able to send information back to Earth, but they are still carrying their copies of the Golden Record. If they encounter an alien ship in the far future, the Voyagers may be able to pass on humanity's message.

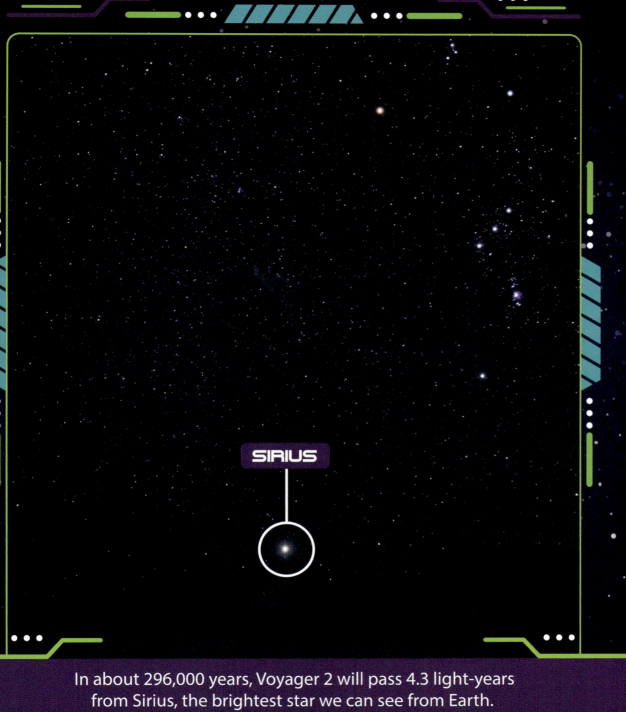

In about 296,000 years, Voyager 2 will pass 4.3 light-years from Sirius, the brightest star we can see from Earth.

THE NEXT PROBE

When the Voyager probes were built in the 1970s, they were very advanced technology. They were made to last at least five years, but they were built so well that they have lasted nearly 10 times as long. As their shutdown nears, NASA is already thinking about a new probe—one that will be made for a long trip from the start.

The project, which is known simply as Interstellar Probe right now, will be designed to go straight to interstellar space and to travel much faster than the Voyagers. Scientists want the probe to do things such as take a picture of the outside of the heliosphere and visit dwarf planets. The timeframe for this project is not set yet, but what is certain is that NASA is committed to further exploration of interstellar space.

NASA KNOWLEDGE

The Interstellar Probe is **tentatively** set to launch sometime in the 2030s, but that is only an idea. NASA will not know the timeframe until engineers begin building the probe.

A dwarf planet is smaller than a planet but larger than a moon. The most famous is Pluto (shown here). Only five dwarf planets have been officially recognized in our solar system, but scientists believe there could be hundreds or thousands more.

GLOSSARY

corrupt: To change from the original or correct form or version.

distribute: To spread out across a space.

environment: The natural world.

escape velocity: The speed at which an object must travel to overcome a planet's gravity and enter outer space.

heliosphere: The region of space that is affected by the sun or solar wind.

interstellar: The space between stars.

spectrometer: An instrument that measures the wavelengths of different kinds of light.

tentatively: Subject to change.

thruster: An engine that produces thrust (forward movement) by discharging a jet of fluid or a stream of particles in the opposite direction (backward).

unique: Special or one of a kind.

FOR MORE INFORMATION

BOOKS

Knapman, Timothy. *The Book of Blast Off!: 15 Real-Life Space Missions*. New York, NY: Magic Cat Publishing, 2023.

Ringstad, Arnold. *Space Missions*. Mankato, MN: The Child's World, 2021.

Schaefer, Lola M. *Explore Space Probes*. Minneapolis, MN: Lerner Publications, 2023.

WEBSITES

NASA SpacePlace: Voyager
spaceplace.nasa.gov/search/Voyager
This website includes games, art projects, and information about Voyager 1 and 2.

NASA: Voyager Golden Record
voyager.jpl.nasa.gov/golden-record/whats-on-the-record
Explore the pictures and sounds that were included on each copy of the Golden Record.

Our Universe for Kids: Voyager Program
www.ouruniverseforkids.com/voyager-1
Learn more interesting facts about Voyager 1 and 2.

Publisher's note to educators and parents: Our editors have carefully reviewed these websites to ensure that they are suitable for students. Many websites change frequently, however, and we cannot guarantee that a site's future contents will continue to meet our high standards of quality and educational value. Be advised that students should be closely supervised whenever they access the internet.

INDEX

A
auroras, 16

C
cameras, 8
Cassini-Huygens, 17
cosmic rays, 10, 21

E
escape velocity, 7

F
fuel, 6, 9, 26

G
Ganymede, 21
Golden Record, 12, 13, 26
gravity, 6, 7

H
heliopause, 19, 24
heliosphere, 18, 19, 24, 28

I
instruments, 4, 8, 9, 10, 18
interstellar medium, 20, 21
Interstellar Probe, 28, 29
interstellar space, 4, 6, 15, 18, 19, 20, 28
Io, 14, 16

J
Jupiter, 4, 6, 7, 14, 15, 21, 25

M
magnetic fields, 10, 14, 16, 21
magnetometer, 10, 16

N
NASA, 4, 5, 13, 20, 22, 23, 24, 26, 28, 29
nebula, 21
Neptune, 4, 6, 15, 16, 17, 25

P
"Pale Blue Dot," 15
plasma, 8, 10, 11, 18, 20
Plasma Wave System (PWS), 18, 20
Pluto, 15, 29

R
radio dish, 8, 9

S
Saturn, 4, 6, 14, 15, 25
Sirius, 27
solar flares, 25
solar minimum and maximum, 24, 25
solar wind, 16
spectrometers, 8, 10

T
Titan, 16, 17
thrusters, 8, 9

U
Uranus, 4, 6, 14, 15, 25

V
volcanoes, 14, 16, 17